The WayOut Bunch

Created by
Jenny Tulip and Dawn Smith

The Way Out Bunch books feature genuinely endangered living animals. The information in each book is collated from known facts about them.

All paper used comes from sustainably managed forests

I'm Curious Cat on an adventure to see
what the animal within these pages can be.
So let's read together and have a good look
and we shall find out by the end of this book.

The World
N
W
E
S
Brazil

Curious Cat is off to explore
the continent of South America.
There are lots of countries here in which
this animal lives, one of them is called Brazil.
"Help me choose the Brazilian flag,
and I will wear it on my hat."

Ecuador

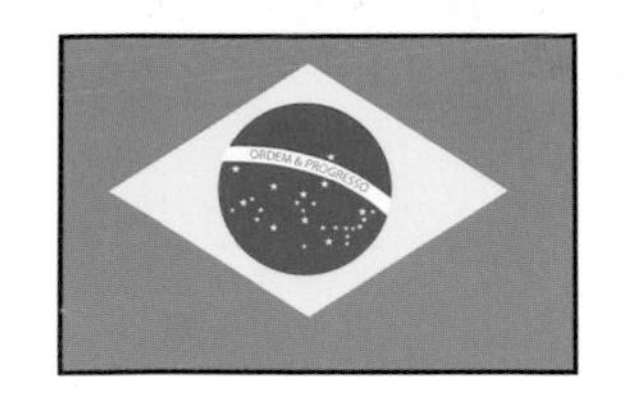

Brazil

Venezuela

Argentina

Suriname

French Guiana

Colombia

Paraguay

Guyana

My two little eyes are round and bright
but I can't see a lot, I have terrible sight.

"I wonder what on earth this animal is?
Do you think it can be one of these?"

On top of my head I have ears round and small,
I can hear every sound, I'm aware of them all.

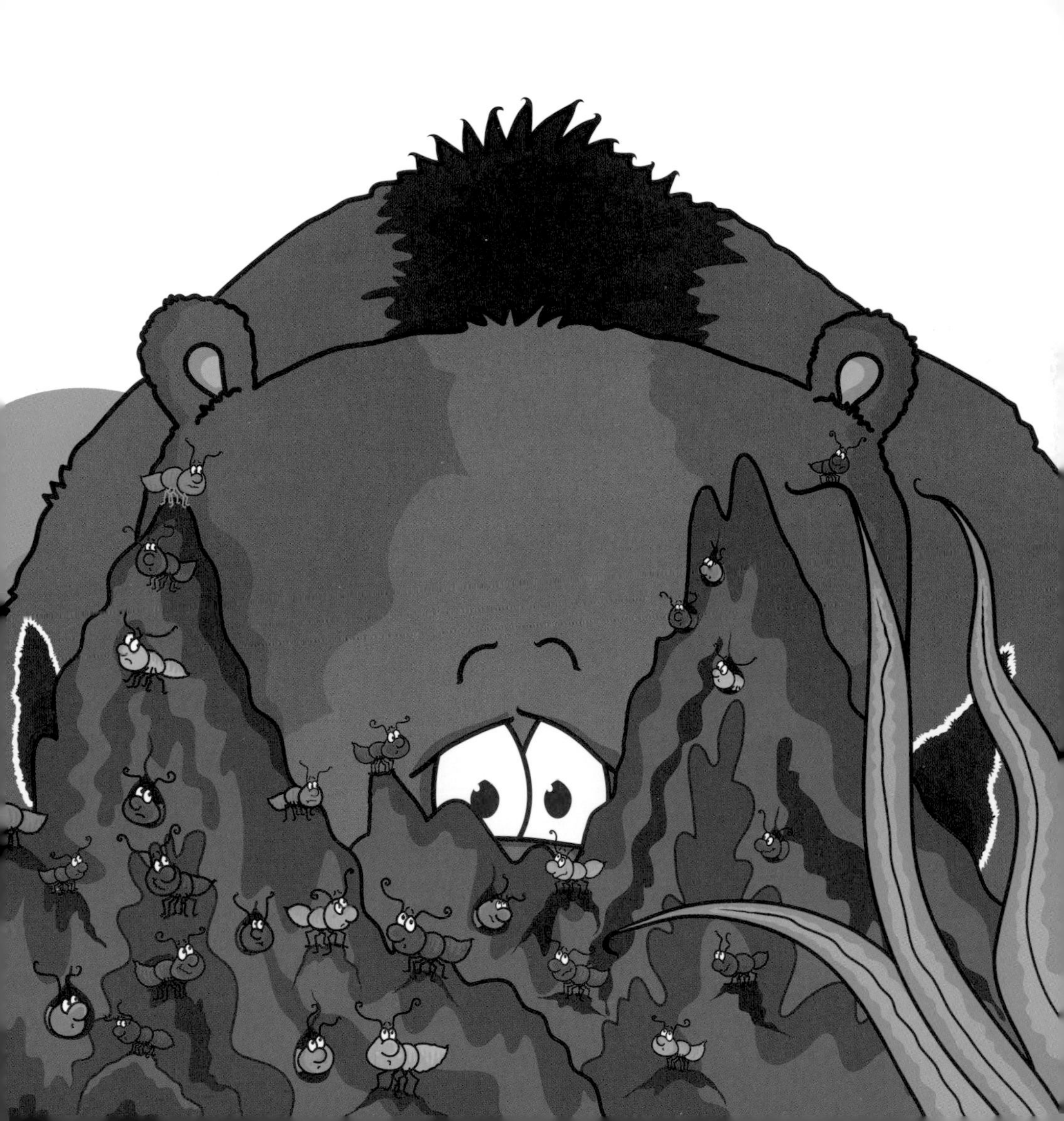

"It can sometimes be quite hot
where this animal lives.
What clothes would you wear when it's hot?"

On both my front feet I have very sharp claws,
But they're tucked up behind when I walk on all fours

"I wonder what this animal likes to eat.
Can you remember?"

These animals are rare, there aren’t many around,
but where there are ants a few may be found.

I'm a Giant Anteater and you'll surely agree,
I'm the strangest of creatures you ever did see.

Did you know.....

The average length of the human tongue, including yours, is 10 cm. Anteaters' tongues can be as long as 60 cm!

They flick their tongue in and out up to 150 times a minute to suck up ants and termites like a vacuum cleaner.

Anteaters have no teeth

They can eat up to 30,000 insects a day.

Because ants and termites are not a very nutritious food, the Giant Anteater moves slowly to conserve energy.

To protect themselves when threatened, they rear up on their hind legs using their tail to keep balance.

They can run up to 50 kph for short distances.

They are very strong swimmers.

At the end of their snout is a very small nose and mouth.

Baby anteaters are carried on their mother's back for a year or more after they are born.

If the baby falls off the baby will make a high-pitched grunt.

Giant Anteaters have a rubbery skin which protects them from the bites and stings of some species of ants and termites.

Jaguars and other large cats hunt and kill Giant Anteaters. But the biggest threat they face is from humans destroying their habitat.

If you would like to find out more information on endangered animals and how to help them, visit these websites:

WWF-UK - www.wwf.org.uk
The Edge programme - www.edgeofexistence.org
ARKive, images of life on Earth - www.arkive.org

A percentage of our profits will be donated to relevant charities.